MYSTIC
SEAPORT®

Photographs by Steve Dunwell
Introduction and text by Lisa Brownell
Published by Mystic Seaport Museum Stores
Mystic, Connecticut

Cover: The ship *Joseph Conrad*   *Overleaf:* Two historic vessels, the *Joseph Conrad* and the *Charles W. Morgan,* dominate the waterfront.

"Time and tide for no man stay."

The tides have risen and fallen for eons, relentless as the passing of time. In a place along the Mystic River, the tide may go in and out, but time itself appears to be almost suspended.

Mystic Seaport Museum has collected a thousand lost moments from American history and assembled them to tell the story of a nation's links to the sea. By preserving the ships, artifacts, buildings and skills of the last century, the Seaport provides a window (or rather a porthole) to the world of the past.

But the past is not just a memory here. It is tangible, a place filled with the sights, sounds and smells of a coastal New England village.

Most of the great sailing ships are gone now — lost at the bottom of the sea, burned, abandoned or scrapped — but a few are safe at their berths at Mystic Seaport. The last wooden whaleship in America, the *Charles W. Morgan*, is the centerpiece of the museum. Built in 1841, and a veteran of more sea voyages than any vessel of her kind, the *Morgan* is a symbol of all the Seaport strives to achieve in the field of maritime preservation.

Like a treasure chest, Mystic Seaport has been slowly filling with the bounty of the sea since its modest beginnings as the Marine Historical Association in 1929. In that inauspicious year in the nation's economy, three local residents, Carl C. Cutler, Edward E. Bradley and Dr. Charles K. Stillman, made the first move to create a nonprofit institution that would preserve the rapidly disappearing traces of America's maritime history.

Why Mystic, Connecticut? This small community, located a few miles inland from Long Island Sound, is as closely linked to the sea as the Mystic River itself. The area was named "Mistick" or tidal river by the Indians who inhabited the nearby woodlands in pre-colonial times.

Mystic was still a sparsely settled river valley when some of its earliest settlers began to shape its destiny through fishing and shipbuilding. While some continued to farm the land for their livelihood, others turned their sights to the sea.

The lack of a significant harbor prevented Mystic from becoming a major trading port such as Boston or even nearby New London, but nevertheless it was home to several dozen whaleships in the years before the Civil War. But the tiny settlement was to produce a legacy which would outshine any community of its size: Mystic was destined to build great ships.

Some believe vessels were being constructed on the shores of the Mystic River as early as the mid-1600s, but most evidence points to a later date, soon after the Revolutionary War. In the century that followed, numerous shipyards would rise and fall along the river,

reaching their peak of productivity for a 30-year period in the mid-1800s.

Scores of great ships were launched during that time: transport ships and steam vessels that carried men and arms during the Civil War; clipper ships that brought would-be prospectors to the California gold fields and carried tea from China; and yachts that set new records for ocean racing.

One of the most prominent and productive of these shipbuilding yards was situated on the present site of Mystic Seaport, which was largely marshlands in that period. The George Greenman and Co. yard, established in the late 1830s, soon became the largest shipbuilding operation in the state, setting new standards with the construction of ships as large as the 1,679-ton clipper ship *David Crockett,* one of the fastest ever built.

Mystic yards continued to produce schooners and other smaller vessels up until the First World War, but the glorious days of the mid-1800s would never return.

In 1929, the three founders of the Marine Historical Association launched their new organization with little more than a small collection and no place to exhibit it. That would change two years later when the association was presented with the land and buildings of the Mystic Manufacturing Company, near what is now the Seaport's north end.

One of the mill's smaller buildings became the organization's first exhibit hall, and in 1931 the first historic vessel was donated to the association: the sandbagger, *Annie.*

Despite her unassuming name and unusual appearance, *Annie* was a champion among racing yachts of her kind. Built in Mystic in 1880 with a sail plan that was double the length of her hull, the boat required a crew of at least a dozen and a supply of 50-pound sandbags to keep her from capsizing on every tack.

From this lone exhibit hall and one vessel, Mystic Seaport was to attain a size of nearly 40 acres with a collection of 60 buildings and more than 300 historic watercraft. The growth of the museum was steady, but in the 1940s, two imposing newcomers would change the course of the museum forever: the whaleship *Charles W. Morgan* and ship *Joseph Conrad.* Both served as catalysts for expansion. Quite simply, the ships required a 19th-century setting to properly interpret and present them. And as the decades passed, the ships demanded specialized skills and labor to preserve them.

Mystic Seaport grew not only in size but also in the scope of its purpose and programs.

In November 1941, a battered old relic was towed up the Mystic River. This once proud ship, now the sole survivor of the fleet of Yankee whaleships, almost sank in the river before reaching her berth at the maritime museum.

A century earlier, the *Charles W. Morgan,* named for the Philadelphia Quaker who was her first principal owner, was launched in the Acushnet River near New Bedford, Massachusetts. In the 80 years that followed, the whaling bark would cross more miles of ocean and make more profits for her owners than any other whaleship on record.

Measuring 111 feet from stem to stern, and capable of carrying 319 tons, the wooden vessel brought four generations of Yankee whalemen to the farthest reaches of the globe. Her 37 voyages, each a tale of adventure and tedium, hardship and success, were charted to whaling waters from the South Seas to the Arctic. New Bedford was home to the *Morgan* from 1841 to 1886. A voyage begun in that year brought the whaleship back to port in San Francisco, where she sailed from for 18 years. The ship did not see New Bedford again until 1906.

The *Morgan* was similar in appearance to the hundreds of wooden whaleships that once made up the Yankee fleet, but her record set her apart from all the rest. The profits from her maiden voyage alone exceeded the cost of building the ship, and her life-long earnings would add up to $1.4 million. Like any working whaleship, she served not only as a factory for processing oil, but also as the "supertanker" of her day, carrying as many as 2,700 barrels of oil to light the lamps of New England homes and lubricate the machinery of the budding Industrial Revolution. Baleen and whalebone were used for everything from ladies' corset stays to umbrella handles. And ambergris, that exceedingly rare substance from a whale's intestines, was the base for fine perfume.

Although whaling was prohibited by the United States government in 1971, the industry itself had already begun to die out following the discovery of petroleum in 1859. By 1921, the year the *Morgan's* active service came to a close the American whaling industry was becoming obsolete. Many of the vessels that had flanked the *Morgan* at the New Bedford wharves were long gone by that time: burned, sent to the bottom of the sea or destroyed during the Civil War.

Already an anachronism, the *Morgan* was used as the set for two early silent films in the 1920s: *Down to the Sea in Ships* with Clara Bow, and *Java Head.* For more than a decade, the vessel remained on exhibit at the South Dartmouth, Massachusetts estate of Colonel E.H.R. Green, grandson of one of the ship's major owners.

Following the death of the colonel, the fate of the ship once again was left undecided. The 1938 hurricane had heavily damaged the ship, and the economic climate of the times was not conducive to the care of this centenarian. A few short weeks before the country was plunged into war by the attack on Pearl Harbor, the *Morgan* arrived at Mystic Seaport. Here, because of the weakened condition of her hull, she was berthed in a sand and gravel base as she had been at Colonel Green's. She remained this way for the next 32 years.

With a boat or ship of any size, maintenance and repairs are a perpetual responsibility, and the *Morgan* is no exception. Work on the vessel has been continuous since her arrival, but her beautifully restored condition today is largely the result of a 15-year effort which began in 1969. In that year, it was recognized that the *Morgan's* true home was in salt water, and that in order to save her, she must be returned to a floating condition.

Work began soon after to reinforce the ship for its next challenge, and the ship was floated free again in 1974. A few years later, the major job of "retopping" the vessel began. This 19th-century practice consisted of replacing a vessel's major planking and framing above the waterline. A new deck of yellow pine also was laid, in the same manner it would have been accomplished while the ship was in service. The *Morgan* was raised on a lift dock for several years while work continued.

Every hour of labor hand hewing a timber, driving a trunnel or bending a plank was matched by an hour of research taking place behind the scenes. Since the ship was built without blueprints, as was the practice in that era, finding the details of her original construction was often likened to unraveling the plot of a detective story.

Thanks to continuing efforts to maintain the ship, Seaport visitors now can walk the decks of the *Morgan,* go below to view the blubber room and the sailors' living quarters in the fo'c'sle, and descend into the cavernous hold where giant oak casks are stored and serve as ballast. The iron hull of the ship *Joseph Conrad* sets her apart from most of the vessels at the Seaport, which are made of wood. The 103-foot-square-rigged ship was launched in 1882 and sailed under three flags: the Danish, English and American.

Originally named the *Georg Stage,* the vessel was built to serve as a training ship for youths in the Danish merchant marine, carrying crews of 80 boys in the Baltic and North seas. The darkest hour of her career came in 1905, when she was rammed by a British freighter off Copenhagen and sunk to the bottom of the sea, taking the lives of 22 young mariners. In a matter of days, however, the ship was raised and repairs were begun.

In 1934, when the ship was retired from service and

headed for the scrapyard, a famous mariner, Captain Alan Villiers, bought the ship from the Danes. To mark the beginning of a new life for the vessel, Villiers rechristened the ship the *Joseph Conrad,* in honor of the author who celebrated the sea in his many works. Under the British flag, Villiers skippered the *Conrad* on a circumnavigation of the globe that lasted two years.

Following her sale by Villiers in 1936, the *Conrad* was used as a private yacht by millionaire Huntington Hartford before being presented to the U.S. Maritime Commission three years later. Once again, she fulfilled her original intention as a training ship, this time in the waters off Florida.

After the end of World War II, the *Conrad* was transferred to the Seaport by an Act of Congress in 1947.

Although visitors are welcome to walk the beautiful teak deck of the *Conrad,* her living quarters below decks are a dormitory reserved for the use of young people who participate in the Seaport's Mariner Training Program. Now, more than a century later, the *Conrad* still fulfills the purpose for which she was built.

In marked contrast to the hulls of the *Morgan* and *Conrad* is the sleek schooner *L.A. Dunton,* at 123 feet, the longest of the Seaport's vessels. The fishing schooner was designed for capacity, seaworthiness and speed and was probably the last of her kind to be constructed without an engine.

Built by Arthur Story in Essex, Massachusetts in 1921, the *Dunton* sailed for more than 30 years out of Boston and St. John's, Newfoundland. During the warmer months, the schooner fished for halibut, and, in the winter, freighted salt fish to market. The fishing boat made about 20 trips each year carrying 10 dories and a crew of 20 fishermen, captain and cook. Life onboard a fishing schooner was demanding and hazardous, but fishermen enjoyed better wages than most seamen through sharing of the profits from each voyage — a reward that frequently outweighed the risks.

Acquired by Mystic Seaport in 1963, the *Dunton* was restored to her original appearance, eliminating many of the alterations which had been made in her later years of operation. Now Seaport visitors may board this graceful vessel which is only one of a handful left in the world today.

Another fishing boat which came to berth in the Seaport's collection is the *Emma C. Berry,* one of the oldest surviving commercial fishing vessels in the country. Launched in the Mystic River in 1866, this Noank Smack later was converted to a schooner which worked as both fisherman and coastal freighter. She too was restored to her original condition at the museum.

And, in a class of her own, is the 1908 steamboat *Sabino* which carries visitors from the Seaport on short cruises from May to October and can be seen at dockside throughout the winter. *Sabino* is the last coal-fired passenger steamboat operating in America, evoking a bygone era of elegance and charm as she steams along the waterfront. Powered by the original 75-horsepower Paine compound engine, the small white steamer is a tribute to the work of many at the Seaport who have preserved her fine condition.

This work can be observed in the duPont Preservation Shipyard, a facility unique in the world today, where craftsmen combine 19th-century shipbuilding techniques with a few 20th-century innovations. Visitors can watch ongoing work on the vessels on or off the 375-ton capacity lift dock, as well as viewing a variety of operations in the main shop from the visitors' gallery.

On a smaller scale, boatbuilding continues on a daily basis in the museum's small boat shop. Here, using traditional methods, significant small craft types from America's past are reproduced for display or for sale. Funds from such sales support the museum's small craft programs and research. In two small craft exhibits elsewhere on the grounds, outstanding examples of small watercraft are highlighted. From Rob Roy canoes to the steam launch *Nellie,* each vessel brings the story of its past back to life again.

In addition to the boats Americans worked and played in, the Seaport also chronicles boats that were built for the sheer joy of competition. Yachting history is a major element at the museum. The collection includes the original New York Yacht Club building, artifacts from the schooner *America* that launched the America's Cup tradition, videotapes of historic races, and paintings and models of famous yachts.

And then there are the boats themselves, most notably the schooner-yacht, *Brilliant,* built in 1932 and still one of the most beautiful on the water today.

Although Seaport visitors most often find themselves gazing at the waterfront, there is just as much to be seen on land, beginning with the streets of the museum's 19th-century exhibit area. Most of the buildings on this point of land are original structures that were brought to the Seaport during the past half-century and restored. Each represents a vital element in the social and economic framework of a coastal New England town during the period from 1814 to 1914.

A typical walking tour of the village begins at the Buckingham House, distinguished by its enormous central chimney and open hearth. Across the way is the Tavern, a favorite gathering spot for whalers and other seamen, and the first bank to be constructed in Mystic, a solid granite structure dating to 1833.

The 1820s Burrows House nestles comfortably

alongside the cooperage or barrel maker, an important shoreside industry in the last century. The Mystic Press turns out the latest broadsides and notices on a Liberty Clamshell Platen press, manufactured in 1880. A mast hoop shop, nautical instrument store and ship-smith also are in this area, the latter being an original structure that once stood on the wharves of New Bedford. Here, ironwork for the rigging of the Seaport's own ships is made today.

The chandlery, the department store for seagoing people in the past, occupies the same first level of the large white building housing the sail loft and rigging loft, all essential operations to support any maritime venture. Hundreds of miles of rope for ships' lines were once manufactured at the Plymouth Cordage Company ropewalk which now stretches next door. The 250-foot building is less than a quarter the size of the original structure, which was longer than the Empire State Building is tall.

From the western end of the ropewalk, visitors emerge to find the trim white lighthouse, a reproduction of an early Nantucket original and a landmark which is unmistakable in widespread photographs of the Seaport.

The village has hours more of exploration in store for the curious: fisheries exhibits, a shipcarver's shop, drug store, general store, one-room schoolhouse and a Children's Museum, brimming over with the toys, books and games of yesterday's children.

The heart of the museum will not be found in the artifacts or ships, however, but in the people who breathe life into the Seaport every day. Aside from interpreting the many facets of each exhibit, Seaport staff give outdoor demonstrations of a variety of maritime skills. A squad of young workers sets and furls the sails on the larger ships, demonstrates how to handle a whaleboat, split a cod fish or save a shipwreck victim from a half-submerged mast by means of the "breeches buoy rescue."

Although outdoor activities may be subject to the weather, indoor activities continue in all seasons. The shipcarver patiently coaxes a new figurehead or other carving from a block of native wood while, two doors away, the shipsmith hammers red hot ironwork at the anvil. A sailmaker is measuring a sail for the mainmast of the *Conrad* as a clockmaker makes a fine adjustment to an ancient ship's clock. A loom is neatly threaded to make a rug while a cook is preparing a stew in a kettle over an open hearth. And, while a shipwright is pounding a trunnel into the side of a ship, a model maker may be making his ship's repairs with a pair of tweezers and a magnifying glass.

At least once a day, a museum "roleplayer" crosses the last barrier between past and present by appearing in 19th-century costume and manners. A visitor may find himself discussing a sea captain's latest trip around Cape Horn or the current views on temperance as he comfortably settles into the time warp of Mystic Seaport. In a similar vein, a chanteyman may bridge the gap with a rousing chorus of a sea chantey from the porch of the tavern or under a ring of trees.

At some point during a visit to the Seaport, most people take in the half-hour show at the Planetarium, which simulates the splendor of the night sky at any hour of the day. Here they learn about the role of the stars in guiding mariners throughout the ages. A 30-minute film program containing historic footage of an actual whale hunt, and dramatic scenes of a storm at sea is screened several times each day.

A visitor who stops to inquire "Where is the museum?" as he wanders through the grounds, will usually be informed that he is standing in the middle of it. There are, however, exhibits which conform to the traditional notion of a museum as a place to view rare artifacts and art on display. Perhaps the best overall view of the Seaport's many themes can be found on the first floor of the Stillman Building. Here, the exhibit "New England and the Sea" presents a microcosm of many parts of the maritime experience: among them, early exploration, trade, whaling and fishing. The upper levels showcase dramatic collections of scrimshaw and ship models. The models range from a ship six feet in length to one only half an inch long, rigged with human hair.

In the Wendell Building, the original building with which the Seaport launched its career, great figure-heads gaze over the heads of visitors as they once did over thousands of miles of ocean. The adjoining Mallory Buildings record the achievements of one of Mystic's most prominent shipbuilding families, and on the other side of Anchor Circle, the captain's quarters of the "Cape Horner" *Benjamin Packard* provide a vivid reminder of a long-since vanished world.

Like a giant iceberg, the museum can display only a small part of its actual volume. The collections which lie in reserve provide both support for those on view and insurance for the future, storing thousands of units of information about the past. The museum's role in this respect, is similar to the keepers of a time capsule.

Although the Seaport has grown in size and complexity since it was created, some of the best of what it has to offer cannot be described in print. It is the simple things that are most keenly felt and remembered, perhaps the smell of salt from the river or a gentle breeze that awakens the desire to "go down to the seas again." And, at Mystic Seaport, anyone still can find "a tall ship and a star to steer her by."

———

Lisa Brownell

1

1. Whaleboats and rigging of the *Morgan* frame the view of the
   square-rigged ship *Joseph Conrad*.

2. A rare double figurehead, these sisters once graced the bow of a
   19th-century ship. The vessel's name is unknown.

3. One of the Seaport's most diverse exhibits, New England and the
   Sea introduces varied themes of the maritime past.

4. Joseph Conrad, whose writings gave us some of the most lasting
   and powerful images of the sea, is immortalized in this figurehead.

2

3

4

9

1

2

1. The coal-fired *Sabino* cruises past the *Conrad,* recalling an era on
   the water when steam power eclipsed sail power.
2. The museum's larger vessels are hauled for periodic maintenance
   and restoration on the shipyard's lift dock.
3. In this seagull's view of the Seaport, the *Sabino* heads downriver.
   The museum's duPont Preservation Shipyard is at the upper left.

1

2

3

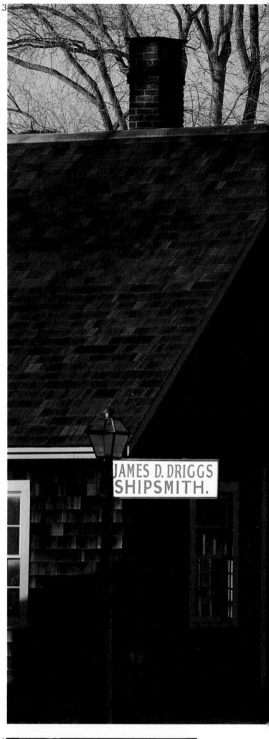

4

1. Sails sewn in lofts such as this one were tested by winds around the globe.
2. A steady hand and sturdy leather palm keep an ancient craft alive at the Seaport.
3. Charles Mallory built this sail loft in Mystic in the 1840s, before he became one of the most prominent shipbuilders and owners in the state. The Driggs Shipsmith building once stood on the New Bedford wharves.
4. These massive blocks, made from lignum vitae, were built to endure. The lives of the crew and the safety of the ship depended on the faultless operation of the rigging.

1. On a summer evening, the setting sun casts a glow on the iron hull of the *Conrad.*

2. Lawrence Anderson works in the tradition of shipcarvers whose figureheads and other carved decorations were meant to distinguish and bestow luck on a vessel.

3. Looking west from the rigging of the *Morgan,* the masts of the *Conrad* loom tall. The latter is actually one of the smallest full-rigged ships ever built.

1. The schoolhouse and Stone's Store are at the heart of the museum's village area, a collection of authentic 19th-century structures.
2. Six generations of schoolchildren learned to read and write in the Boardman School, originally located in Preston, Connecticut.
3. Florence Butten, better known as "Granny," shares her memories of her Mystic girlhood and brings to life the contents of Stone's Store.
4. Salt was a staple on any grocery list in the 1800s. These sacks line the shelves of the Stone's Store, a business typical of the era 1870 to 1880.
5. In stores such as this one, the buyer could find everything from groceries to hardware, and garden seeds to cigars.

3

4

5

Overleaf: A member of the outdoor demonstration squad secures a line on a yard of the *Morgan.*

1

1. Once the home of a prosperous shipbuilder and his family, the
   Thomas Greenman House was built on its present location in 1842.

2. Victorian order and ornament in the Greenman parlor recall the
   domestic life and styles of the Gilded Age.

3. Ivory sewing items line the interior of a lacquered sewing table
   from China.

2

3

1. Lines of type are locked into position in preparation for inking in the Seaport's Print Shop, where century-old equipment still operates.

2. The Liberty clamshell platen press, run by a foot pedal and wheel, opens and closes in an action similar to that of a clamshell.

3. A high-powered double telescope aims at the waterfront from the window of the Nautical Instrument Store.

4. Clocks at sea were used for more than telling time; they were essential in determining position at sea. Sextants, chronometers, quadrants and other nautical instruments are repaired and displayed in this exhibit.

3

4

1

1. Shipbuilding yards once occupied the present site of Mystic Seaport Museum, launching scores of vessels in the mid-1800s.

2. Young people in the museum's mariner training program make their maiden voyage aloft to set a sail.

3. Even a sturdy 28-foot boat could be destroyed by the fluke of a whale. Here, Seaport staff demonstrate ways of handling a whaleboat as it was done during the chase.

24

2

3

1. This shipping office first opened for business in New York City in 1841. Samuel Thompson's Nephew and Co. were agents for both cargo and passenger service to England.

2. A carved gold eagle gleams on the transom of the *Morgan,* now a National Historic Landmark. Built in New Bedford in 1841, the bark is the last wooden whaleship in America.

3. The Mystic Bank was the first to be built in the community and one of the oldest in the state of Connecticut.

1

4

1. The granite bank contrasts with the weathered shingles of the cooperage, reflecting an architectural diversity that is typical of the New England waterfront.

2. The work of the cooper was invaluable at sea or ashore. A well-made cask kept cargo and catch intact during long sea voyages.

3. Ships' lanterns, standard equipment on sailing vessels, could be purchased with other supplies at a chandlery.

4. Patterns from the past are repeated on the hand-operated looms of the Edmundson House.

28

29

Overleaf: Wooden figureheads such as these from the *Great Admiral, Donald MacKay,* and *H.M.S. Orlando* can be traced to identified vessels. The origins of many others, such as this Woman with Beads, remain a mystery.

GREAT ADMIRAL   58.1095
The ship GREAT ADMIRAL was ex-
ceptionally well built, along the
lines of the medium clipper, by
Jackson of East Boston in 1869.

1. Traditional designs such as this 14-foot cedar Rushton rowing boat, which dates to the 1880s, take shape under the hands of skilled craftsmen in the Small Boat Shop.
2. Giant timbers used in the restoration of Seaport vessels are cut to size at the shipyard's sawmill.
3. A shipyard worker does maintenance work on a Noman's Land Boat. Built in 1882, this seaworthy craft was named for a small island near Martha's Vineyard.
4. At the turn of the century, Nathanael Herreshoff designed this triple expansion steam engine to power a yacht tender at a top speed of eighteen knots.
5. *Quill II* is a tender once used on a cruising yawl of the same name. Powered by a one-cylinder gasoline engine, the tender was built in 1905.

33

1. Gardens and shade trees extend throughout the museum grounds.
2. A 7,000-pound anchor from an early 19th-century British warship rests in front of the Meeting House, a former Seventh-Day Baptist church.
3. Taverns such as this one were more than just a place for a seaman to quench his thirst. They also served as the social hub of a waterfront community.
4. Spouter Tavern is named for the fictional inn where the narrator Ishmael of Melville's *Moby Dick* first·joined the company of seafarers.

4

1

1. Home port to history, the Seaport covers seventeen acres along the Mystic River. It is the largest maritime museum in the nation.
2. The bandstand on the village green is the stage for concerts on summer evenings and a favorite daytime meeting place.
3. The early 19th-century Burrows House is sandwiched between the Print Shop and the cooperage.

1. This unpretentious cottage served as the first headquarters for the New York Yacht Club in the 1840s. Later, under this same roof, yachtsmen planned the challenge which sparked the America's Cup tradition.

2. The oyster sloop Nellie is docked alongside the Thomas Oyster House where the shellfish were opened and packed in ice for delivery.

3. Capstans and anchors cast their shadows near the entrance to the chandlery.

1

1. Snow trims the outline of an icebound Seaport, etching a peaceful image from days gone by.

2. Launched in 1891, *Nellie* once dredged Long Island Sound for oysters from fall until spring. Her working days over, she now spends the winters safe at her berth.

3. Winter light accentuates the classic lines of the Meeting House.

4. The sparsely decorated interior of the Fishtown Chapel reflects the hardworking, pious nature of the people who once knelt to pray here.

40

3

4

2

41

1. William Quincy, a master modelmaker, must do the work of a shipwright, carpenter, rigger and sailmaker, all on a miniature scale. Here he works on the *Charles W. Morgan.*

2. Carved from beef bone by a French prisoner in an English jail, this model represents the *Queen Charlotte.* The actual four-decked British ship was built in 1790.

3. *Sea Witch,* a clipper that once held the record for the fastest passage from China to America, is shown in all her glory in this 64-inch model.

4. This scrimshaw masterpiece captures the action of the Battle of Lake Erie. A companion piece illustrates the Battle of Lake Champlain.

5. A demure gentlewoman, whose image was copied from a fashion journal of the time, adorns a five-inch sperm whale tooth.

BATTLE OF LAKE ERIE.—PERRY'S VICTORY.

1. A warm hearth can always be found in the Buckingham House, where cooking and chores revolve around the kitchen fireplace.

2. A kitchen window provides a backdrop for a simple still life.

3. Fall colors blaze alongside the somber hues of this pre-Revolutionary home.

1

2

1. Dozens of herbs were kept on hand in an early pharmacist's office.
2. In a seaport community, the druggist stocked medicines and supplies for mariners on their voyages and also tended to the needs of those ashore.
3. The leather-bound medical guides in this doctor's desk date to 1842.
4. Pill machines such as this one were used by some pharmacists as late as the 1940s for preparing special remedies.

3

4

Rowing creates a reflective mood on the Mystic River.

Photographs ©copyright 1985 by Steve Dunwell
This book ©copyright 1985 by Mystic Seaport Museum Stores
and Fort Church Publishers, Inc. may not be
reproduced in any form, in whole or part without
the written permission of the publishers. Photography
may not be reproduced in any form without the
written permission of Steve Dunwell.
Edited by James B. Patrick
Designed by Donald G. Paulhus
Printed in Japan
ISBN 0-939510-01-4
Distributed by Mystic Seaport Museum Stores,
Mystic, CT 06355